Hey, Stop!

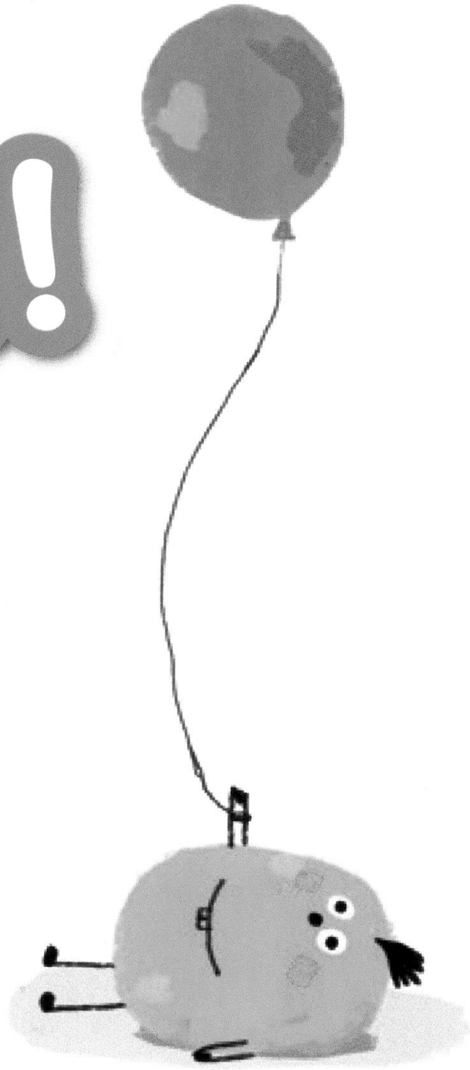

Story by Alison Hawes
Illustrated by Sophia Touliatou

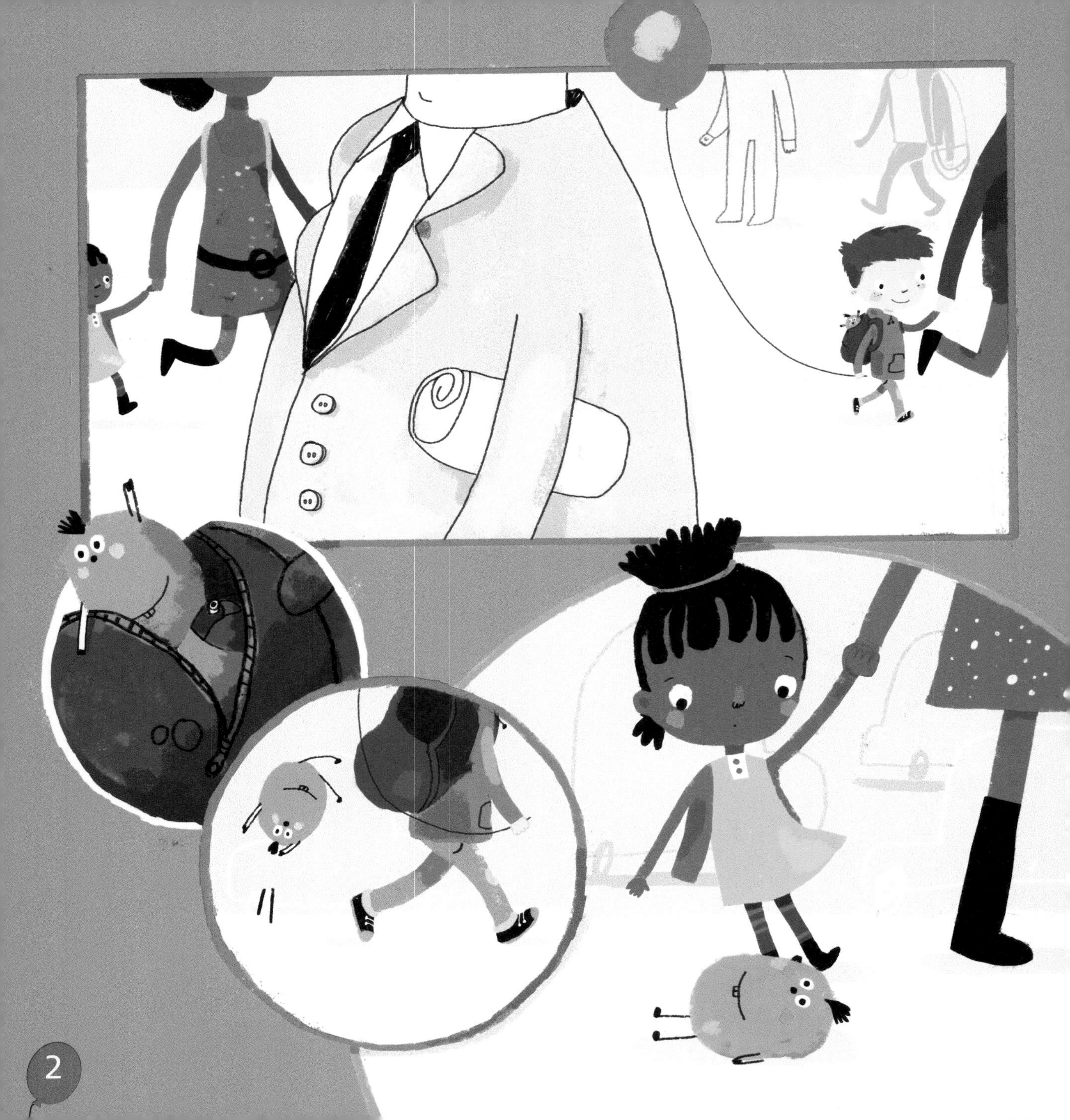

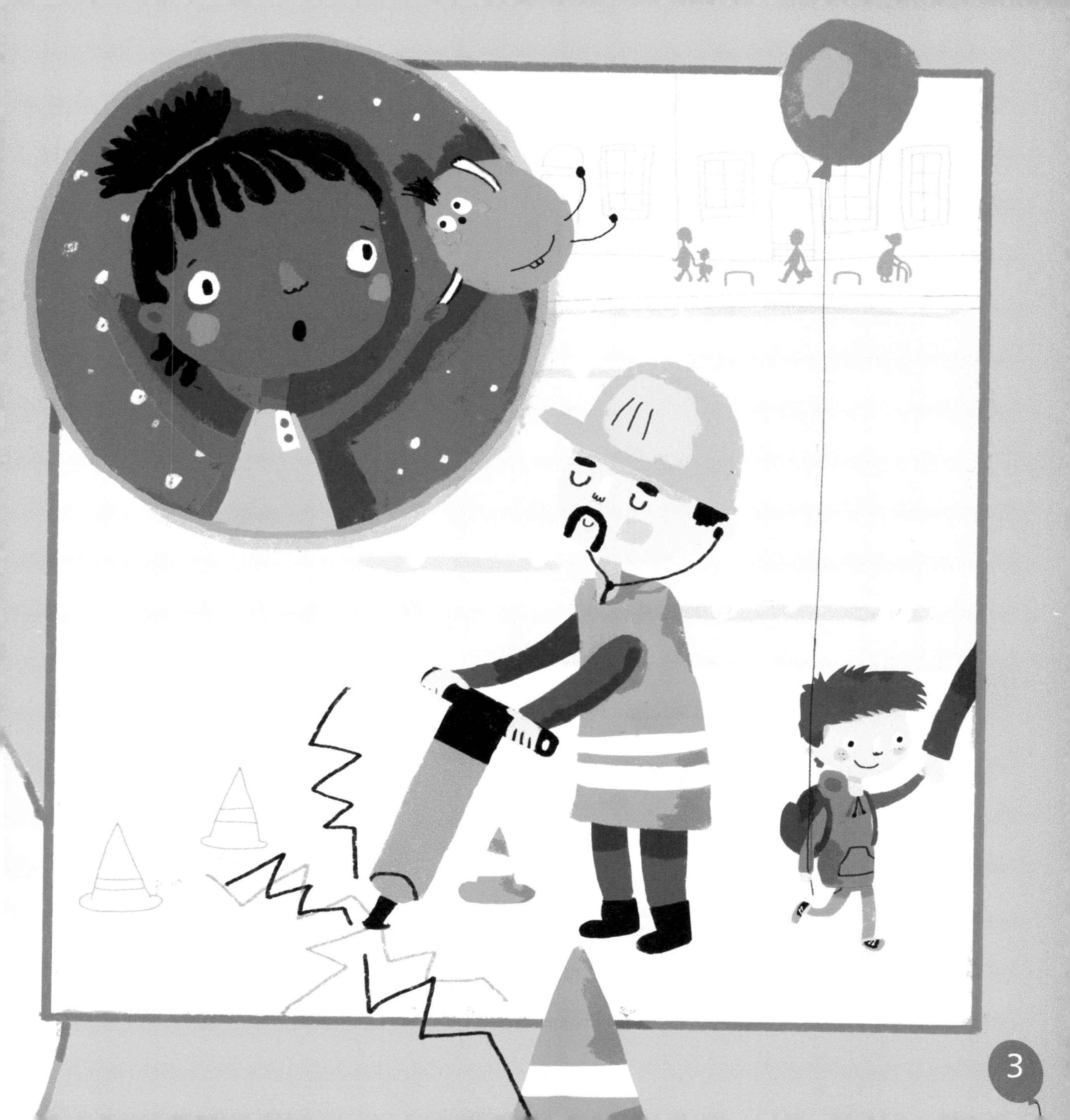

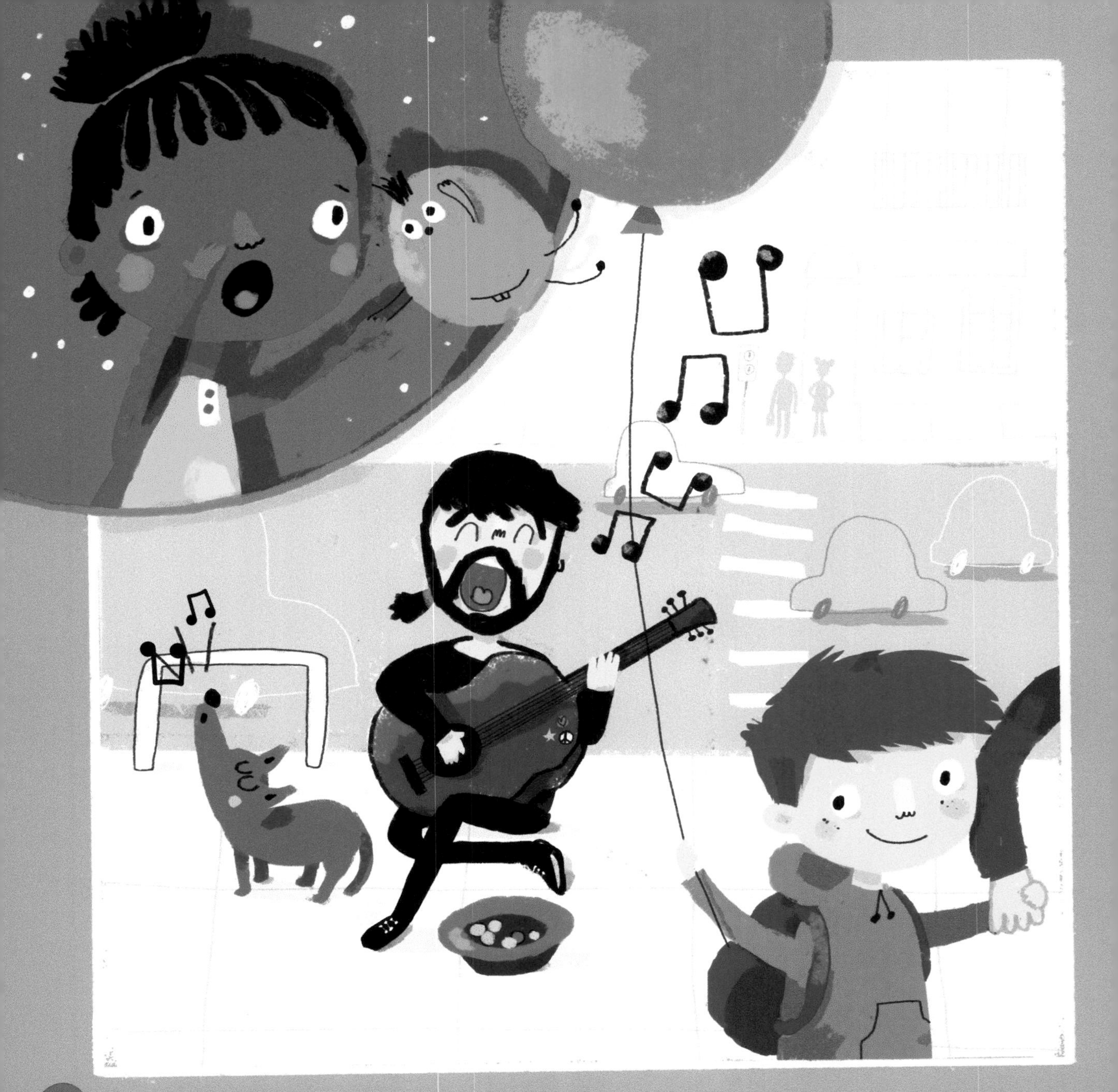

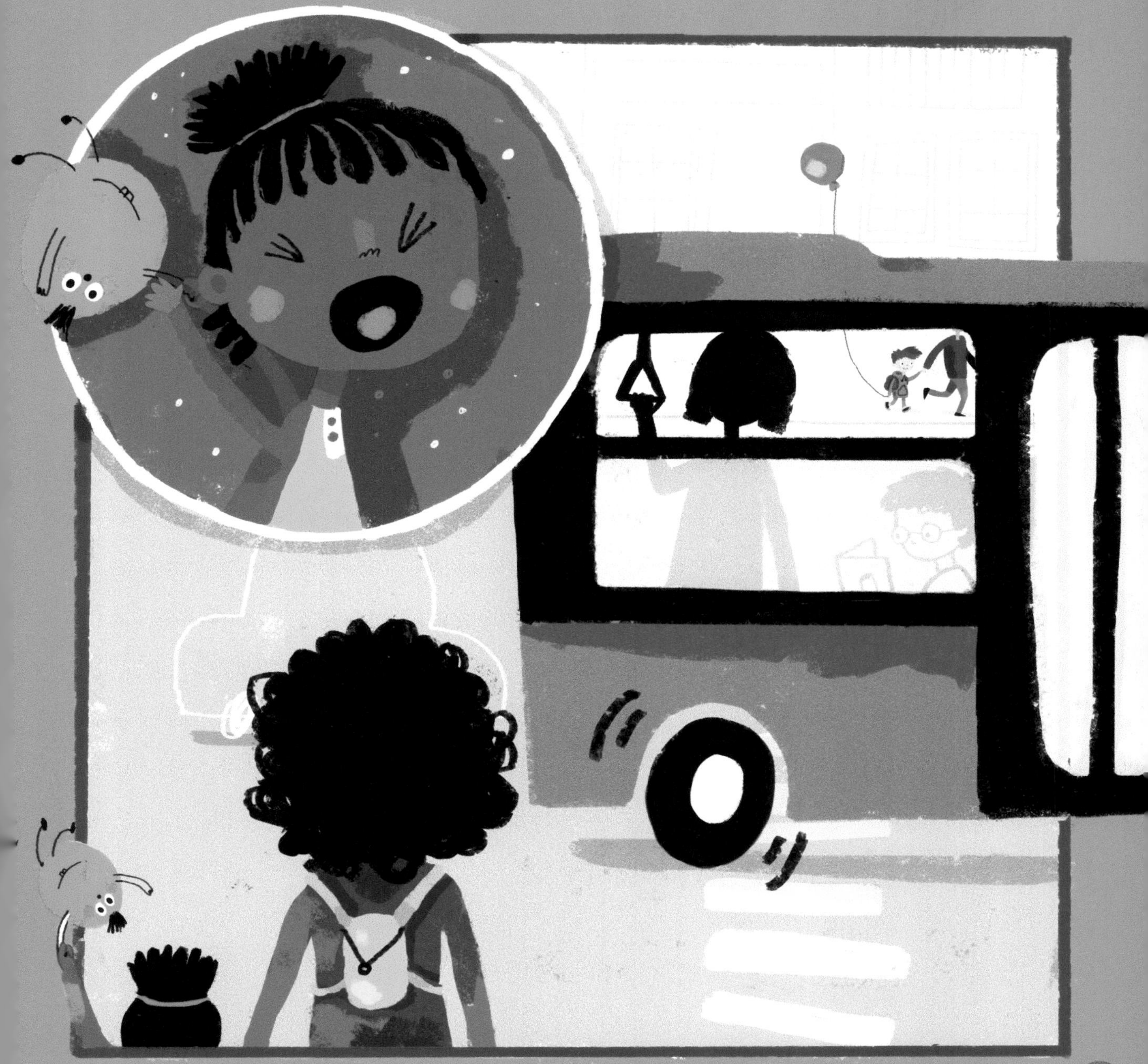

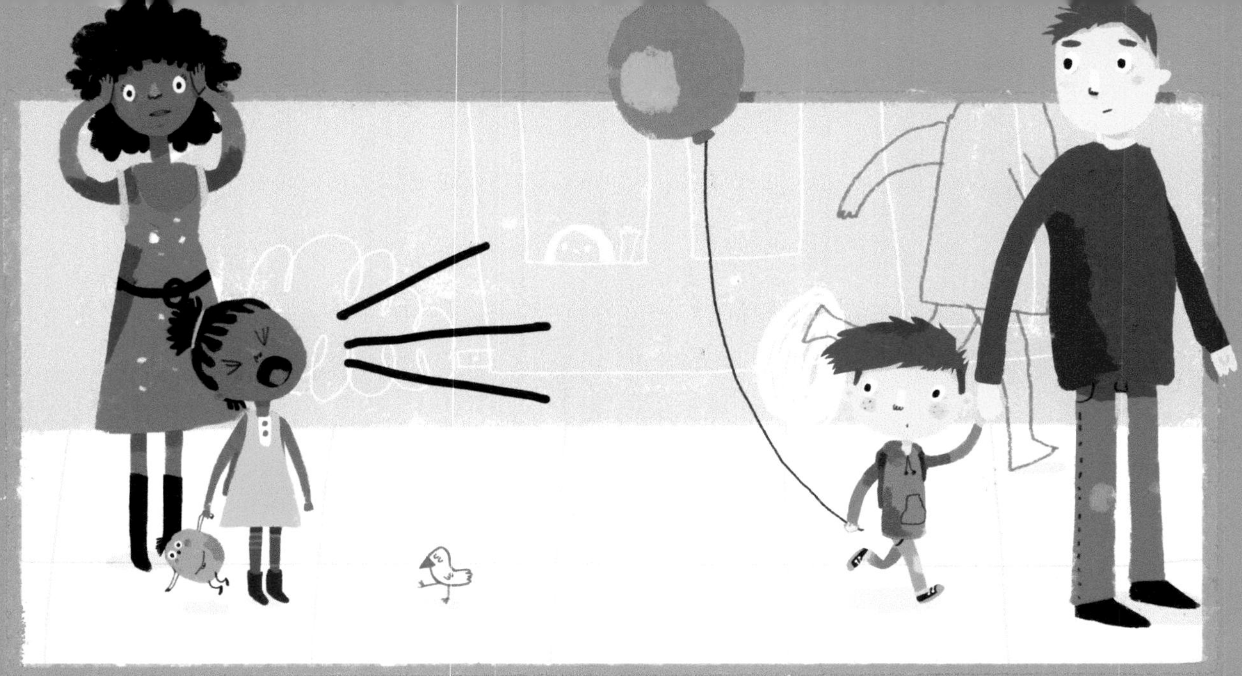

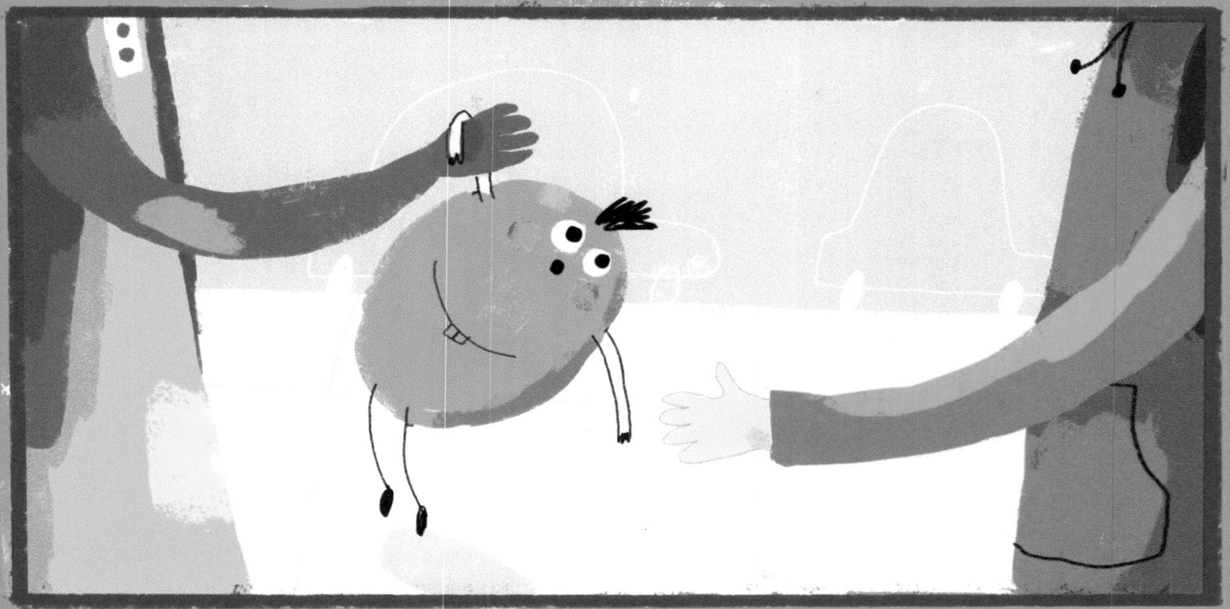

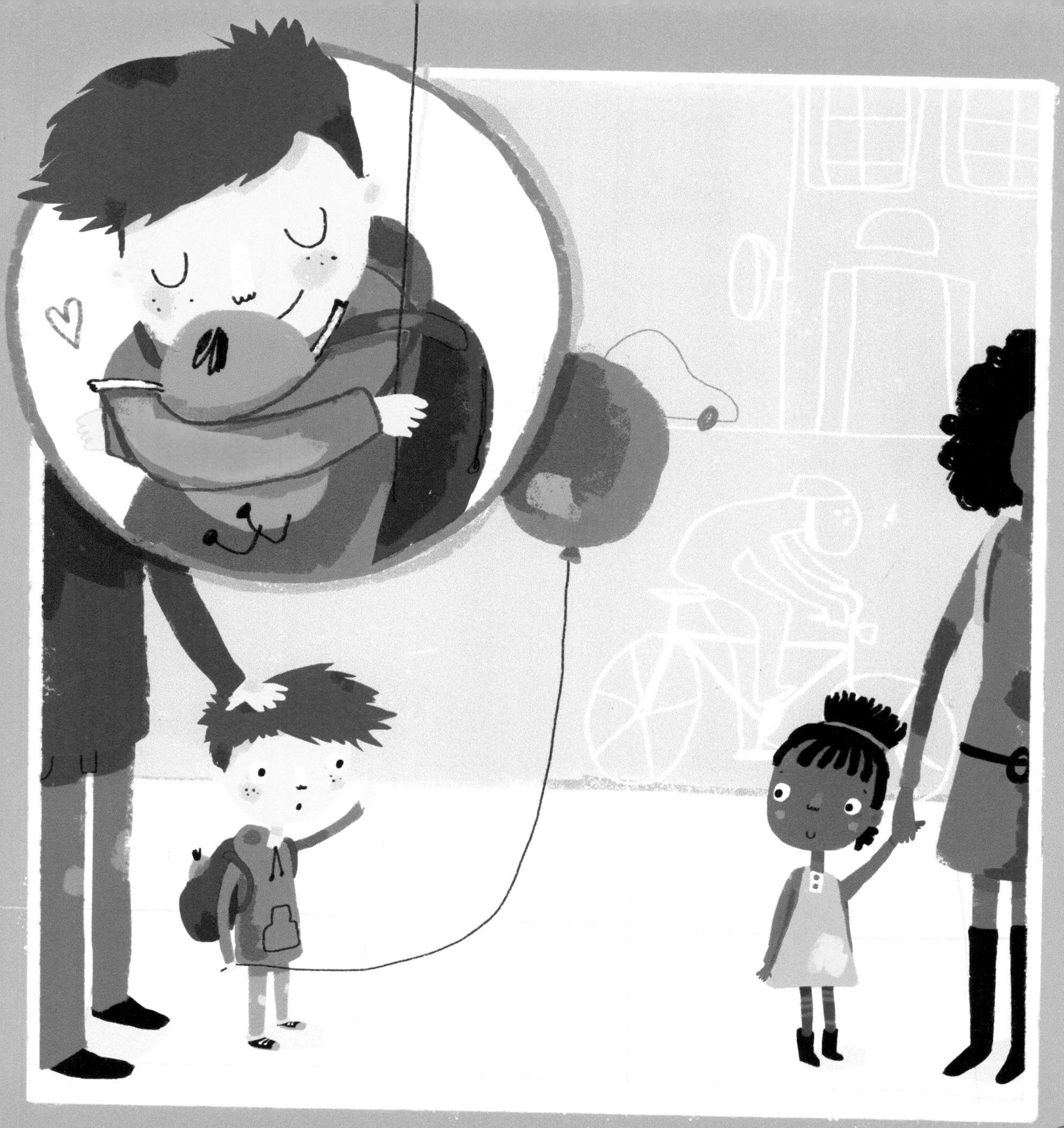

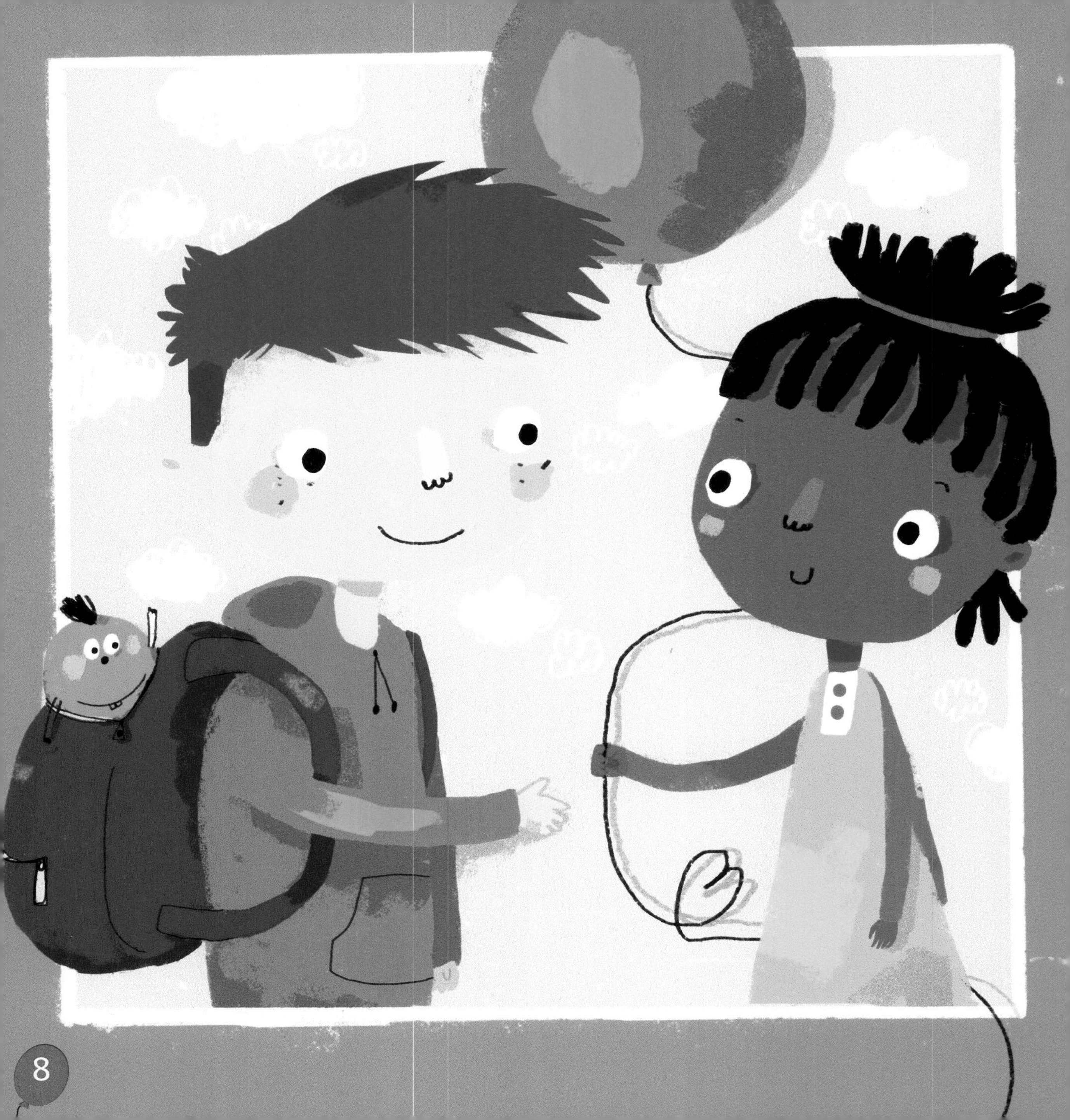